CONTENTS

snapping-turtle
guide

Copyright © 2001

ticktock Publishing Ltd UK
http://www.ticktock.co.uk

LIVING IN HARMONY

Tribal people in South America have lived in harmony with their rainforest environment for thousands of years — only taking from the forest what they need to live. This ecological balance is now being threatened and tribespeople are gradually leaving their rainforest home.

HABITATS

A habitat is any place where a group of organisms can live. Ponds, streams, rock pools and moorland are all habitats. Large habitats like forests are made up of many smaller habitats. Each species of wild plant and animal has adapted to survive in a particular habitat. Penguins, for example, are ideally suited to their environment. They have flippers that allow them to fly through the water in pursuit of fish, while thousands of tiny feathers and a layer of fat under the skin allow them to cope with the intense cold of the Antarctic.

BIODIVERSITY

All around the world, ecologists are identifying and counting every kind of living organism. This helps us to understand the amazing variety of life on Earth and how living things have changed with time. So far, ecologists have identified and described more than one-and-a-half million different species. They include all kinds of plants and animals, fungi, bacteria and other simple forms of life. No one knows the total number of species on Earth, but it could be as many as 10 to 15 million. New species are discovered every week. This incredible variety of life is known as biodiversity.

NIGHT VISION

Many flying insects, including most moths and praying mantises, are active only at night. In order to study the numbers and varieties of these insects, ecologists sometimes use special light traps. These traps give off a faint bluish light which is hardly visible to the human eye. Insects find it irresistible because the light has a wavelength to which their eyes are very sensitive. The insects are caught, identified and recorded, and then released.

SURVEYING VEGETATION

Ecologists spend a great deal of time mapping vegetation. Vegetation can change for natural reasons or because of human interference or damage. For forests, deserts, mountains and other areas which are very large or difficult to access, ecologists may use photography from an aircraft or a satellite to help them with their mapping. Certain types of satellite photographs show different plants and vegetation in different colours as in this image of Hawaii.

TRICKS & TECHNIQUES

To be good at their work, ecologists need to observe, measure and record all the different aspects of the area they are studying. They must count or map the plants and animals of different species, and record where they grow, their movements and how they live, feed and breed. Then they must measure the physical features of the environment, such as soil moisture and acidity, temperature, wind speed, light intensity and humidity. By comparing all these measurements and observations, ecologists can decide what conditions particular species need to survive, and what effects certain changes will have on the plants and animals in an ecosystem.

WATCHING WATER

Testing water for pollution is an important job for an ecologist. Sooner or later the water that we have used in our homes, schools and factories finds its way into a river or the sea, usually after it has been cleaned in a sewage works. But not all water is cleaned and, since polluted water is not always easy to spot, ecologists regularly take samples of water from lakes, rivers, streams and the sea. Back in the laboratory, they analyse the water to see what chemicals it contains. Ecologists also regularly check on the wildlife living in the water because any changes can mean the water is polluted.

FISHY BUSINESS

Ecologists sometimes tag fish they have weighed and measured in order to track movement and growth. If the fish is caught again later, they will know how far it has travelled and how much it has grown. Sometimes a tiny radio transmitter is fitted under the skin of a fish, or fixed to its tail. The fish is returned to where it was first caught and tracked by a boat equipped with a radio receiver that picks up signals from the fish. Sometimes similar transmitters are used to track birds and larger land animals.

FOOD DETECTIVES

It is important for an ecologist to know what foods wild animals eat. However, clues are not always obvious to the naked eye. Ecologists have devised a technique called faecal analysis to help them study an animal's diet. They collect the fresh droppings and put them into a preservative. Then, by examining tiny fragments under a microscope, they can see what the animal has been eating.

ALL CREATURES GREAT & SMALL

This ecologist is using a small trap called a Longworth trap to see how many mice, voles, snakes and shrews are living in an area of woodland. Some nesting material and food is placed in the box part of the trap. Then, when a small animal enters, it steps on a trip wire which shuts the door of the trap. The next day the animal can be identified, weighed, measured and then released. If a large number of such traps are set in a line across a wood or area of heath or grassland, they give a clear picture of what small animals are living there.

PLANT LIFE ON EARTH

There are more than 380,000 different kinds (or species) of plant in the world, in environments ranging from high mountains and desert plains to under the sea. In fact, wherever there is water, light and reasonably warm conditions, plants are almost certain to grow. Plants are vital to us because they help to make the air fit for us to breathe. Our food comes from plants, or from animals that eat plants. We also use plants in many other ways, such as for wood and to make medicines, fabrics and perfumes. Even the paper used for this book came from plants.

REMARKABLE RICE

Rice is a tropical grass cultivated by people. It provides the main cereal diet for half of the world's population in Asia, and Central and South America. Rice is unique among the various cereals in that it is usually cultivated in standing water in fields called paddy fields. The hollow rice stems allow oxygen down to the waterlogged roots of the plant. The flooded fields encourage the growth of tiny blue-green algae, which are able to turn nitrogen from the air into substances that the rice plants can use as a fertilizer. The algae can make as much as 100 kilogrammes (45 lb) of fertilizer for each hectare of field.

PHOTOSYNTHESIS

Green plants do not have to eat. They are the only living things that can make their own food from simple raw materials found in the air, water and soil. They use carbon dioxide gas from the air and water from the soil, from which they extract mineral salts. The energy needed to join these materials together comes from sunlight, which is trapped by a green substance called chlorophyll. Plants arrange their leaves so as to catch as much light as possible.

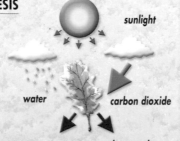

sunlight

water

carbon dioxide

plant produces sugars and starch

plant produces oxygen gas

ONE-HIT WONDERS

Sunflowers, like many other plants, live for only one growing season, then produce seeds and die. They belong to one of the largest families of flowering plants, with over 25,000 species. These include daisies, asters, ragwort and dandelions. The plants of this family are unusual in that what appears to be one flower is really a large number of small flowers. Sunflowers are cultivated for their seeds from which cooking oil is obtained. Some of the oil is also used to make margarine, soaps, paints and varnish. Sunflowers turn throughout the day so that they are always facing the sun.

SEEDS & CONES

Most of the larger plants we are familiar with grow from seeds. Most seeds come from flowers, but a smaller number of plants have their seeds in cones. These include pine, larch, spruce, fir and yew. They are often called conifers and most of them are large trees. The giant redwood trees of California (*right*) are enormous conifers that grow to heights of more than 110 metres (366 ft). They are also the oldest living things on Earth, reaching ages of up to 3,000 years. Their vast size is partly due to the fertile soil and humid conditions of the west coast of North America where the trees grow in river valleys.

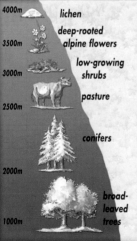

4000m	lichen
3500m	deep-rooted alpine flowers
3000m	low-growing shrubs
2500m	pasture
2000m	conifers
1000m	broad-leaved trees

ON THE LEVEL

Different plants can survive at different levels. On a mountain there is plenty of light for plants to grow, but biting cold winds mean that only the toughest species can survive at high altitudes. On most tall mountains, forests of broad-leaved trees such as beech and oak clothe the lower slopes, giving way to conifer trees farther up. Above a certain height (the tree-line), it is too windy and cold for trees to be able to survive. The trees give way to tough grasses, mosses, lichens and a few deep-rooted flowering plants.

SCIENCE EXPLAINED: STOMATA

Leaves are riddled with hundreds of tiny holes called stomata. It is only possible to see stomata with a microscope. Carbon dioxide gas enters the leaves during the process called photosynthesis, the name given to the way in which green plants make their food. Oxygen gas produced as a waste gas goes out of the plant through these holes. All living things (including humans) need this oxygen to breathe. Water also evaporates from the plant through the stomata, so a plant has to keep taking up water through its roots to avoid wilting.

Many snakes are too slow to chase their prey, so instead they hide and wait for a meal to pass. Different kinds of snake kill their prey in different ways. Snakes, such as this rock python from Africa (*right*), are called constrictors. They wrap themselves around their prey and squeeze hard. The prey soon runs out of breath and dies. Other snakes, such as adders and puff adders, poison their prey. They bite them with teeth called fangs that drip a poison (known as venom) into the wound. Snakes can open their jaws very wide and swallow their prey whole. A big meal such as this gazelle might last a python for several weeks.

THE ADAPTABLE AVOCET

Birds come in all shapes and sizes and many live in specialized environments. The avocet frequents seashores and salt marshes where it feeds on shrimps, ragworms, water snails and other small invertebrates. In clear water the avocet pecks at its prey, but in muddy water, where it cannot see clearly, it traps its food by feel. The bird holds its upturned bill slightly open under water, sweeping it from side to side. Unlike most wading birds, the avocet can swim well if it gets out of its depth because it has partially webbed feet.

GRIZZLY FEAST

The brown or grizzly bear of Alaska, Canada and western North America is the largest of the seven species of bear in the world. Although brown bears have a reputation for being ferocious, they usually avoid humans. They are solitary animals, wandering the bleak land in search of food. Their life is one of feast and famine. In summer and autumn there are fish, carrion and ripe fruits, nuts and berries to eat. But for at least three months of the winter, the bears fast in their dens. During this time the female brown bear also gives birth and nurses her young.

SCIENCE EXPLAINED: HERBIVORES VS CARNIVORES

All animals have to eat in order to survive, and their bodies are adapted to suit the kinds of food they eat. Animals that eat plants are called herbivores. Larger herbivores have long, sharp front teeth that enable them to bite off pieces of plant, while their back teeth are flat and broad for grinding up tough pieces of vegetation. Animals that eat other animals are called carnivores. The larger ones have sharp, pointed teeth and strong jaws for grabbing and slicing through flesh.

ANIMAL LIFE ON EARTH

Scientists like order and, if they can, they like to put things into groups. They group animals in a process called classification. The animals with a backbone are called vertebrates, and there are about 45,000 different vertebrates alive today. Animals without backbones are called invertebrates and they are an even larger and more varied group. Ninety-five per cent of all the animals on Earth are invertebrates. Altogether there are about 950,000 different species ranging from one-celled animals to the giant squid, which may be up to 20 metres (66 ft) long. Invertebrates can be found on land, in water, in the soil, in the air and even in the snow of the polar ice caps.

LIFE IN THE OCEAN

Nearly three-quarters of the Earth is covered by water, a habitat which supports an abundance of life. On the surface are floating animals and plants, while below a wealth of animal and plant life can be found, from corals and underwater plants to fish, whales and turtles. Even in the depths of the ocean, which go down to incredible depths of over 11,000 metres (36,000 ft), life has found a way. Down at this level, the sunlight vital for photosynthesis cannot penetrate, so creatures get their energy from the Earth itself. Deep down in the ocean, huge sections of the seabed are constantly on the move, producing hot water which gushes out of underwater vents. Bacteria feed on the chemicals released, and are in turn eaten by fish and other animals.

CLASSIFICATIONS

Ecologists put the thousands of different kinds of animals into groups to study. Each group contains animals that share several key similarities. The most fundamental division is between vertebrates and invertebrates, but ecologists use many other categories when classifying animals.

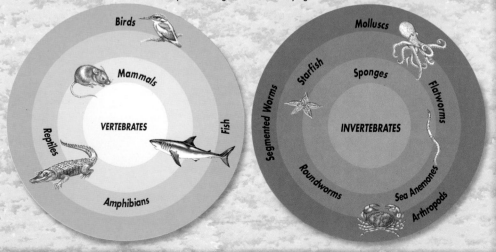

Birds
Mammals
Reptiles
VERTEBRATES
Fish
Amphibians

Molluscs
Starfish
Sponges
Flatworms
Segmented Worms
INVERTEBRATES
Roundworms
Sea Anemones
Arthropods

ECOSYSTEMS

Plants, animals and the environment where they live **form an ecosystem.** An ecosystem can be as small as a pond or as large as an ocean. The whole ecosystem is powered by the sun which provides the energy that lets green plants make their food. Apart from that, almost all the other food and energy supplies come from within the ecosystem. As well as plants, or their dead and decaying remains, all ecosystems contain animals.

Bear

Rabbit

Plants

Plants

FOOD CHAINS

The plants and animals in an ecosystem are linked together in food chains. Green plants make their own food, with the help of sunlight energy, so they start food chains. Animals cannot make their own food, they must obtain it elsewhere. Herbivorous animals eat plants, while carnivorous animals eat other animals. Sometimes a large carnivore will eat a smaller one. The arrows in a food chain mean 'give food to'. Usually as you go along a food chain the animals become larger but fewer in number.

Bobcat

Bear

Hawk

Shrew

Insects

Rabbit

Birds

Plants

Vole

Hawk

Bird

Insect

FOOD WEB

Ecosystems are made up of lots of different food chains, which are often linked to each other. Many kinds of herbivores feed on the same kinds of plants, while many carnivores prey on the same animals. Linked food chains from the same ecosystem are referred to as food webs. Food webs help ecologists understand exactly how the plants and animals within an ecosystem depend on each other.

SCIENCE EXPLAINED: ENERGY & FOOD CHAINS

Plants and animals use food to produce energy, which helps them to grow, move, keep warm and make seeds or have babies. At each step in a food chain, some energy is passed on, but most is lost in the form of heat. This means that much more energy is available at the beginning of a food chain than at the end. That is the reason why food chains rarely have more than four or five links. It is also the reason why no animal specializes in preying on large carnivores such as tigers, jaguars or polar bears.

DECOMPOSERS AT WORK

Plants and animals are always multiplying. If they lived forever, the Earth would soon be overcrowded. Instead, all living things die eventually. But the surface of the Earth is not littered with thousands of dead plants and animals, because a group of living organisms specializes in feeding on dead plants and animals, breaking them down into simple substances. Bacteria too small to be seen without a powerful microscope, fungi, worms, snails, fly maggots and other small animals break down dead bodies and other waste materials into smaller and smaller pieces until all the chemicals in them are released into the soil, water or air. The chemicals can then be used to help other plants to grow.

DELICIOUS DUNG

Despite our view of dung, some small animals, such as flies, beetles and worms find it a wonderful source of food. The yellow dung flies (above) lay their eggs in any crack or crevice they can find in a new pile of dung. The larger and steamier the heap of dung, the more flies it attracts. When the larvae hatch from the eggs they munch their way through the dung, safely removing it out of harm's way.

SCIENCE EXPLAINED: DETRITIVORES & DECOMPOSERS

Ecologists divide the living things that feed on dead animals and plants, dung and other waste materials into two groups. Animals that feed on dead remains, such as beetles and flies (and their larvae or maggots), together with worms, millipedes, snails, slugs and woodlice, are called detritivores. They break the waste materials down into smaller and smaller pieces. It is then left to decomposers, such as bacteria and fungi, to finish the job. They completely break down dead plants and animals, releasing chemicals that other living things can use again.

Plants take root and the roots break up the log.

Woodlice live in the damp holes of rotten wood. In turn they are eaten by spider

Beetle larvae feed on wood.

CASE STUDY: A ROTTING LOG

A few fungi cause plant and animal diseases, but most decompose dead plants and animals and their wastes. In this picture, bracket fungi are growing on a fallen log. But you can only see a tiny part of each fungus, the part that reproduces the fungus by means of spores. Most of the fungus consists of a network of threads, called hyphae. These threads form a tangled web inside the tree trunk slowly dissolving it away. Other decomposers include insects such as snails and slugs, which also eat large amounts of dead plant material. They rasp away the plant fibres with a tooth-covered tongue called a radula, and digest the cellulose, the main chemical in all plants. Their droppings then become available to fungi and bacteria to decompose away completely. Some species of slug are particularly fond of droppings and even eat dog dung. Finally, birds and reptiles, such as frogs, also join in the destruction, chipping away at the rotting log until it eventually disintegrates.

Springtails and other insects feed on dead leaves.

Bracket fungi hyphae slowly dissolve the log.

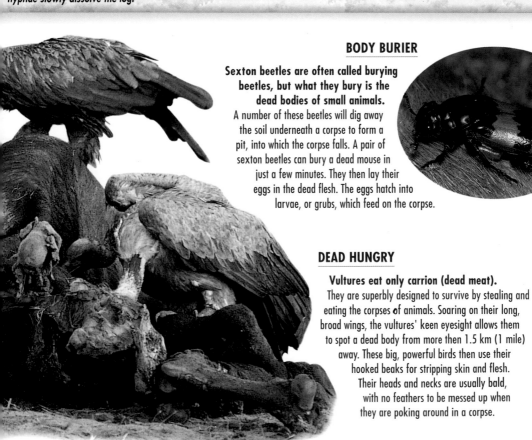

BODY BURIER

Sexton beetles are often called burying beetles, but what they bury is the dead bodies of small animals. A number of these beetles will dig away the soil underneath a corpse to form a pit, into which the corpse falls. A pair of sexton beetles can bury a dead mouse in just a few minutes. They then lay their eggs in the dead flesh. The eggs hatch into larvae, or grubs, which feed on the corpse.

DEAD HUNGRY

Vultures eat only carrion (dead meat). They are superbly designed to survive by stealing and eating the corpses of animals. Soaring on their long, broad wings, the vultures' keen eyesight allows them to spot a dead body from more then 1.5 km (1 mile) away. These big, powerful birds then use their hooked beaks for stripping skin and flesh. Their heads and necks are usually bald, with no feathers to be messed up when they are poking around in a corpse.

CHANGES IN NATURE

Ecologists have discovered that many ecosystems change, often due to the seasons, but there are also less obvious and slower changes. If, for example, a lawn is not mown it will soon be invaded by weeds, the taller ones of which will grow up and choke the grass. The wind will blow the seeds of trees and flowers onto the weedy wasteland. Berry pips from shrubs will be dropped by birds. Some of these seeds and pips will grow, and what was a lawn will become a patch of scrub. Small animals that like these conditions will move in. Eventually the scrub will become woodland. These changes are called a succession, because different species (plant and animal) succeed each other.

SEASONAL CHANGES

In tropical areas, with temperatures constant all the year round, the amount of rainfall determines the season — dry or rainy. Farther north and south, there are four main seasons — spring, summer, autumn and winter. These produce many changes in living things. Most broad-leaved trees lose all their leaves in the autumn and grow new ones in the spring. Some animals migrate to areas, often far away, where conditions are more suitable for feeding or breeding, or both. Other animals, like hedgehogs, bats and snakes avoid the worst seasonal conditions by hibernating.

HELPFUL PONIES

In nature, the changes in a succession towards woodland may be held back by strong winds or very low temperatures. In some cases, repeated fires or grazing by rabbits and other animals can stop the succession at grassland or heathland. On some nature reserves ecologists actually use grazing animals to stop an ecosystem turning into woodland, as on this one in Norfolk, England. Shetland ponies eat any tree seedlings as they appear and so maintain the rare grassy heath vegetation.

A FRESH START

Ecologists rarely have the chance to see how succession occurs on a brand new piece of land. But in 1963 a volcano under the sea near Iceland erupted and formed a new island. The island was named Surtsey, after the Icelandic god of fire. Only months after it was formed, the first seeds and young plants were found on Surtsey. The seeds had either been carried there by the wind or been dropped by birds. After just four years there were 23 species of bird living on Surtsey, 22 kinds of insect and many different species of plants.

RETURNING HOME

The Shenandoah Valley in North America is a specially protected national park, with bobcats (*above*), deer, ravens, owls and a host of other animals forming part of the food web. But it hasn't always been like that. During the 19th century there was hardly a tree in sight. Instead there were farmhouses, cows, pigs and fields of cabbages. Early settlers had cleared all the trees and farmed the land. When the crops started to fail at the beginning of the 20th century, the government decided to abandon the land to nature. Within 20 years the first trees had appeared and now it is one of the wildest places in North America.

SCIENCE EXPLAINED: POLLEN PUZZLES

All flowering plants and conifers produce a yellow dust, called pollen, to help them form seeds. Pollen is produced in vast quantities and scattered over a wide area. Each plant has its own particular shape and size of pollen grains. In certain places, ecologists are able to drill down into the ground and remove a cylinder of the soil. They can identify the pollen grains from different depths and see how the plant life has changed in that area over hundreds or even thousands of years.

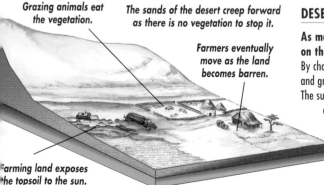

Grazing animals eat the vegetation.

The sands of the desert creep forward as there is no vegetation to stop it.

Farmers eventually move as the land becomes barren.

Farming land exposes the topsoil to the sun.

DESERTIFICATION

As man continues to have an ever greater impact on the planet, the world's deserts continue to grow. By chopping down trees and grazing too many animals on scrub and grassland, people have left soil exposed to the elements. The sun, wind and rain dry out the topsoil, which is then blown and washed away, leaving a desert. Overfarming land can also cause desertification. As the soil is overworked, a desert wasteland is created. This happened in the American Prairies in the 1930s, when a huge area of barren land called the Dust Bowl was created.

WONDERFUL WEEDS

Some of the most adaptable plants are the ones we call 'weeds'. A weed is simply a plant growing where we don't want it to. Weeds can colonize almost any piece of bare or neglected ground. They can flower and produce seeds at almost any time of the year, while some of the most adaptable don't even need to produce seeds. If one tiny part of the root is broken off or left in the soil, it will grow into a new plant.

KNOCK ON WOOD

It would be hard to think of a bird better designed for living in trees than a woodpecker. Woodpeckers feed on wood-boring insects and grubs. Their large feet have two toes pointing forwards and two backwards for gripping tree trunks, while the stiff tail feathers are used like a shooting stick to support its weight. The woodpecker's strong beak is the perfect tool for hammering, drilling and chiselling wood, while special shock-absorbers in its head prevent headaches! Once it has detected an insect or grub, the woodpecker uses its long, sticky tongue to winkle out the tasty food.

ADAPTATION

We are often amazed at how well plants and animals are suited, or adapted, to their environment. The polar bear's white coat allows it to hunt almost unseen in the snowy wastes of the Arctic. The tiny hummingbird is able to suck nectar from tropical flowers because of its long beak and marvellous ability to hover in the air. Some ecosystems are highly suitable for one type of animal or plant and extremely unsuitable for another. On the other hand, some plants and animals are very adaptable and can quickly make a home more or less anywhere.

DESERT FOX

The fennec fox lives in the Sahara and Arabian deserts, where its colour matches the desert sands. Its large ears give off heat, like radiators, and help the fox to keep cool. The large ears also give the fennec fox very sensitive hearing which it uses to locate gerbils, lizards, insects and other prey at a distance. It spends the daytime resting in its cool den, and comes out to hunt only at night when the air is cooler. Then its large eyes help it to see in the dark.

ORCHID ATTRACTION

The bee orchid is a master of deception. The flower of this remarkable plant seems to have a bee resting on it. The 'body' of the 'bee' even feels furry, and it gives off a scent exactly like that produced by a female bee. This fools male bees who fly in to 'mate' with the flower and in doing so become covered with pollen. The insect may then carry the pollen to another flower of the same kind, and this pollination will allow the flower to produce seeds.

CITY LIVING

Living in a city has certain advantages over living in the country for wildlife. The heat produced by people and buildings makes the city a warm place to live in. Buildings provide shelter from the wind and safe places to breed, while food is plentiful in the city's dustbins and rubbish tips. Raccoons have successfully adapted to life in many North American cities. At night they plunder the dustbins and, if they can, cupboards and refrigerators. Some have even discovered how to unstopper wine bottles to drink the contents.

COMPETITION

All living things reproduce, and usually they have far more offspring than can possibly survive. A large female cod can lay 10 million eggs all in one go. If all the cod eggs hatched and grew into adult fish there would not be enough food for them in the sea. In reality, there is what ecologists call a struggle for survival or competition. Living things have to compete for space, nesting sites, food and all the other things they need to survive. Only the fittest and best adapted individuals survive.

SURVIVING THE COMPETITION

Dandelions are one of the most successful and conspicuous weeds. Their feathery fruits, each containing a single seed, are widely dispersed by the wind. Once established, their deep and exceptionally tough roots help them to survive all but the most determined effort by people to remove them. Even a small piece of root left in the ground can grow into a whole new plant within a few weeks. What dandelions cannot compete with is taller and longer-living plants, such as shrubs and trees, which eventually overshadow and kill them.

FIGHTING FOR SPACE

In September, birch trees produce thousands of winged seeds that are scattered by the wind. They take root in forest clearings, ungrazed heathlands and areas that have recently been burnt. The following spring, a mass of tiny seedlings appear. Many are eaten by slugs, millipedes, woodlice, rabbits and other herbivores. Even more of the seedlings die because they are unable to compete with brambles and other faster-growing plants.

Even if the birch seedlings grow into adult trees, they rarely become really large because they are overshadowed by taller trees.

FIGHTING FOR FOOD

Cheetahs are successful hunters, but they are surrounded by would-be food thiefs. With its slim, streamlined body, long legs and supple spine, the cheetah can accelerate from a standstill to 60 mph (100 km/h) in three seconds — faster than any sports car. It can reach a top speed of 70 mph (115 km/h), but once it has caught its prey, the cheetah must rest and cool off before it can eat. During that time it faces competition for its food from lions, hyenas, jackals and even vultures. As a result, cheetahs lose a high percentage of their prey.

MOTHERS' MEETING

Like seabirds, seals spend most of their lives at sea, meeting on land only to breed and moult. By coming ashore, the seals are guaranteed to meet others of the same species for mating, which would otherwise depend on chance meetings at sea. When the seals do come ashore on some lonely beach, they have to compete with each other for mates, and for a space where they can rest and suckle their young.

SCIENCE EXPLAINED: THE HUMAN FACTOR

One major kind of competition which all wild plants and animals have to face is from the rapidly growing human population. As the population grows, more of the wild places where plants and animals live are being destroyed. Hedges, woods and forests are being cut down to make fields, and ponds and marshes are drained for farmland or for building. Roads are built on heaths and moors and houses are built on meadows, while pollution from human activities destroys wildlife homes everywhere.

HABITATS & NICHES

A **habitat is a place where a plant or animal lives.** Some species are found in a variety of habitats, while others are more specialized and can only survive in one habitat. Giant pandas, for example, can only live in the bamboo forests of central China. They have become endangered because large areas of this particular habitat have been cut down. Within an ecosystem there can be many different habitats. Each species ha to find a habitat where it can easily obtain food, and where the levels of water, light and heat suit its way of life. This is called its niche. Because different species tend to have different niches, they avoid competin with each other.

FINDING A NICHE

The gerenuk is a kind of gazelle that has found its own special niche in the grasslands and scrub of East Africa. Gerenuks feed on the leaves of the acacia tree, as do impala antelopes and giraffes. But the impala stands on all fours to eat the acacia leaves, while the giraffe's long neck allows it to reach the leaves up to 6 metres (20 ft) off the ground. The gerenuk has a long neck, and, in order to feed, it stands on its hind legs, with its forefeet touching the bush or tree. It can therefore eat the acacia leaves that are too high for impala to reach and too low for giraffes.

THE HIGH LIFE

The koala of eastern Australia has a very specialized niche as a tree-dweller.
It lives in eucalyptus forests and rarely comes to the ground, where it would be easy
prey for dingoes and domestic cats and dogs. Since it has little opportunity for drinking,
the koala gets its moisture from the leathery eucalyptus leaves. It eats about 1 kg (2.2 lb)
of these each night, and then saves energy by sleeping for up to 18 hours each day —
in a eucalyptus tree, of course!

greenfinch

bullfinch

UNFUSSY FEEDERS

**Some animals are not fussy about what
they eat or where they live.** The red
fox was once confined to wooded country
areas where it was persecuted because it
killed farm and game birds. It was always
an adaptable feeder and in recent years
the fox has moved into town and cities
to take advantage of the cover, lack of
persecution and abundant food available.
Many foxes now live in gardens, wastelands
and railway cuttings, scavenging on waste food.

crossbill

FINCHES

**These three closely related species
of finch do not compete because each
has become adapted to different foods.**
The greenfinch has a strong pointed beak
which it uses to pick open and crack seeds
and cereal grains. The bullfinch uses its short
strong beak to eat the seeds of ash, birch,
nettle dock and berries. When food is scarce,
it turns to the buds of fruit trees and
flowering shrubs. The crossbill uses its strange
crossed-over beak to extract the seeds from
the cones of pines and other conifer trees.

SCIENCE EXPLAINED: A NICHE WITHIN A NICHE

*Species that live in a habitat where food can be scarce often have niches that
prevent them competing with each other. The cormorant and the shag, for example,
are birds that live along the coast and dive for fish. But the cormorant dives deeper,
while the shag concentrates on the fish nearer the surface. Similarly, grey seals and
common seals avoid competition for scarce breeding sites because common seals
tend to breed on sandy beaches and sandbanks during June and July, whereas grey
seals mostly breed on rocky coasts and in caves in the autumn and early winter.*

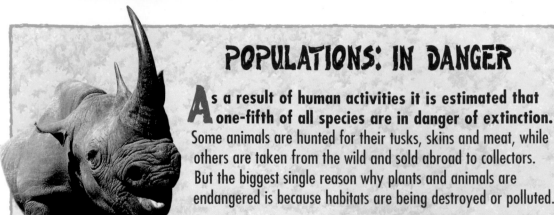

POPULATIONS: IN DANGER

As a result of human activities it is estimated that one-fifth of all species are in danger of extinction. Some animals are hunted for their tusks, skins and meat, while others are taken from the wild and sold abroad to collectors. But the biggest single reason why plants and animals are endangered is because habitats are being destroyed or polluted.

THE RHINOCEROS

There are five species of rhinoceros in the world. All are on the verge of extinction because poachers (illegal hunters) kill them to sell their horns. These are used to make medicines that some people in Asia believe will cure headaches, fevers and other illnesses. Rhino horns are also sold to make dagger handles. In some game reserves in Africa, people are trying to protect rhinoceroses by sawing off their horns so that the poachers leave them alone.

THE BLUE WHALE

The blue whale is the largest animal that has ever lived. It can grow to be over 30 metres (100 ft) long and can weigh more than 160 tonnes (160 tons), about as heavy as 25 fully-grown African elephants. In spite of its vast size, a blue whale feeds on tiny plankton animals. Blue whales were hunted so much in the past for their meat and fat (made into oil) that they nearly became extinct. It is believed that there are only about 6,000 blue whales left today.

RAFFLESIA

At up to 90 cm (3 ft) across and weighing about 7 kg (15 lb), the rafflesia plant has the largest flower in the world. It is also the smelliest and one of the most endangered. The rafflesia is a plant parasite. It has no leaves and takes its water and sugar from the roots of other rainforest plants. The flower is covered in warts and produces a smell like rotting meat to attract the flies it uses for pollination (it is sometimes referred to as the 'corpse lily'). Clearance of the tropical rainforest in Southeast Asia has drastically reduced its habitat.

In general, the animals that produce large numbers of eggs or young are those which do not look after them, or where many of the eggs and young die or are eaten. Fish, insects and amphibians produce hordes of eggs, while birds and mammals, which look after their young, produce small numbers of offspring. Elephants, blue whales and humans usually give birth to only one baby at a time. The parents then spend many years looking after it until it can fend for itself.

POPULATIONS: NATURAL CONTROL

Every living thing can reproduce, some at an alarming rate. A simple bacterium, for example, can split into two every twenty minutes. If there was nothing to stop their growth, after 36 hours a layer of bacteria 30 cm (1 ft) deep would cover the entire surface of the Earth. Fortunately these incredible increases in population do not happen, thanks to natural checks such as shortages of food and space, unsuitable temperatures, disease and other factors.

HOUSEFLIES

Houseflies lay their eggs in dustbins, stale food, corpses and dung. It has been calculated that a pair of them would, if all their offspring survived and bred, be able to cover the entire surface of the Earth to a depth of 14 metres (47 ft) in a single summer. Fortunately cold, wet weather, disease, predators, such as spiders and birds, and people with fly swatters or chemical insecticides all help to keep the number of flies at a reasonable level.

BROWN RATS

Some towns and cities contain more rats than people. Rats cause damage and spread disease. They also breed rapidly from a young age, and one ecologist calculated that a pair of rats could potentially produce 20 million descendants in three years. Fortunately, rats die of disease or starvation. They may not be able to find a mate or a warm, dry nesting site. Many are eaten by owls, hawks, foxes and other enemies; and even more are trapped or poisoned by people.

CASE STUDY: THE GALAPAGOS OIL DISASTER

The Galapagos Islands are a group of 13 major islands and more than 115 smaller ones that lie about 960 km (600 miles) off the coast of South America. In 1885 they were visited by Charles Darwin, inspiring his theory of evolution. Today, the Galapagos Islands are still home to a multitude of plants and animals, many of which are found nowhere else on Earth. However, in January 2001, this unique array of wildlife was threatened when an oil tanker ran aground. Quick work by ecologists helped to avert a major environmental catastrophe.

DISASTER!

During the night of 16th January 2001, disaster struck the Galapagos Islands. The tanker ship *Jessica* ran aground in a bay on the island of San Cristobal. Nearly 900,000 litres (200,000 gallons) of the fuel entered the sea. Some of it was eventually washed up on the beaches of the islands. Fortunately, a combination of hard work by ecologists and good luck with the state of the wind and tides prevented a major ecological disaster.

PREVENTIVE MEASURES

Immediately after the tanker crashed, floating barriers (or booms) were put up around the *Jessica*. These booms are like a row of rubber sausages floating on the water, and they are designed to stop the oil spreading out across the surface. The scientists also put layers of absorbent material on the surface of the sea around the ship to soak up any leaking oil. When the oil spread out beyond the booms and absorbent materials, it was sprayed with chemicals to break it down. At the same time, experts began trying to safely pump the remaining oil out of the tanker.

OIL & WILDLIFE

Oil also destroys the waterproofing on the fur of mammals and the feathers of birds, so that they die of cold unless quickly rescued. So when the tanker crashed, ecologists from the Galapagos research station carried out a quick survey of the wildlife populations likely to be affected by the oil. This included seabirds, who would be unable to fly if they became smothered by oil, and would be poisoned if they attempted to clean themselves. Invertebrate animals were also at risk. They feed by sifting food particles from the water, and both invertebrates and fish breathe with gills. Oil can coat these delicate mechanisms, quickly killing the animal.

24

THE DAMAGE

Amazingly, only about 30 sea lions and 5 sea birds had to be cleaned of the oil. Although most of the ship's cargo leaked out, fortunately the hot sun evaporated a lot of the oil, while the winds and ocean currents carried much of the remainder away from the islands. All the sea cucumbers, sea urchins and many other invertebrate animals, fish and seaweeds in the vicinity of the *Jessica* were killed, but mercifully, the larger animals were much luckier.

THE FUTURE

The Galapagos Islands are home to giant tortoises that occur nowhere else in the world. Ecologists from the Charles Darwin Foundation on San Cristobal, and from the World Wildlife Fund will be making regular checks on these and all other Galapagos species on land and in the ocean for several years. They will pay particular attention to sensitive indicator species, such as algae, sea urchins, sea cucumbers, marine iguanas, sea lions and lava gulls. Any reduction in the numbers of one species could easily have a catastrophic effect on other species.

ALIEN INVADERS

Humans have been responsible for introducing alien species to new regions, sometimes accidentally and sometimes deliberately. Often these alien plants and animals spread out of contro and destroy native wildlife. The best-known species to be accidentally spread is the brown rat. It originated in Asia and spread throughout the world to become a pest to people and their crops, a carrier of disease and a predato It has helped to make extinct at least nine species of flightless bird in New Zealand. Among deliberately introduced species are dogs, cats, rabbits, squirrels, various birds and most other domestic animals.

A REAL CHOKER

In 1884, some water hyacinths from Brazil were taken to a gardening exhibition in New Orleans in the United States. A few gardeners took pieces home to plant in their garden ponds. When the plants grew too big for the garden ponds, they threw the unwanted pieces into nearby streams. Within 90 years, the water hyacinth had spread across much of the southern United States, Australia, India, South Africa and Malaysia. Rivers and lakes were choked with a mat of this plant, one metre (39 inches) thick. The plants blocked out sunlight from the water, so it quickly became stagnant and killed other wildlife.

CULLING THE COYPUS

A native of South America, the coypu was introduced into Britain, other European countries, the United States and parts of Africa, to be farmed for its fur. Some of these giant rat-like animals, each weighing up to 7 kg (15 lb) escaped and became pests. They damaged crops and natural vegetation, as well as the river banks in which they made their burrows. With few natural enemies, the populations of coypu flourished. After intensive trapping and shooting they were finally eliminated from Britain in the 1980s, but remain a pest elsewhere.

GREEDY GOAT

Among the most destructive of the introduced animals are goats. In the 19th century, sailors introduced goats to the Galapagos Islands, to kill for meat at a later date. However, the goats destroyed the habitat of the unique giant tortoises by eating up all the vegetation, while rats (also introduced by accident) ate their young. Today the tortoises are protected by law and have to be bred in captivity on the islands.

RABBITS RUNNING RIOT

Rabbits came originally from North Africa and the countries around the Mediterranean Sea. They were introduced to other countries, including the British Isles, New Zealand, Australia and Chile, to be farmed for their meat. They escaped and bred – like rabbits – devastating crops and young trees. The rabbit shook off predators, such as dogs, cats, foxes, stoats and weasels, and was unaffected by human onslaught with gas, gun, trap and snare. The rabbit populations were eventually brought under control when a virus disease, called myxomatosis, killed millions of them.

SCIENCE EXPLAINED: DISRUPTING FOOD CHAINS

People have been introducing new plants and animals into different parts of the world for hundreds of years. Nearly all our cereals, wheat oats and barley originally came from Asia Minor, while our cattle came from Asia and our chickens from the East. For the most part, these plants and animals were under our control. It is a different matter when plants and animals are set free and left to their own devices. They become a nuisance because they have been taken from their native environment, where they form part of food chains, to places where there are often no natural predators to control their numbers.

MONGOOSE MISCHIEF

In their native homelands, which stretch from Iraq to India and south to Malaysia, mongooses feed on pest animals, including rats, mice, snakes, scorpions, centipedes and wasps. Mongooses were introduced into the West Indies to destroy the rats and snakes that were infesting the sugar cane and other crops. Instead, the mongooses turned to eating the more-easily caught native species, allowing the rats and snakes to flourish. Solenodons, insect-eating animals found only in Cuba, Haiti and the Dominican Republic, are now threatened with extinction by the mongooses.

FAMINE VICTIMS

If too many animals have to survive in one place then they may destroy the vegetation which is keeping them alive. This has happened in the areas around the Sahara Desert. The number of people and domestic animals has increased. The grass has been eaten and trampled on by goats, sheep and other animals so that there is little vegetation left. When it does rain, the water runs in torrents off the surface of the land, before it has time to sink into the soil. The land turns into desert while the people starve to death, unless they receive food aid from elsewhere.

LIVING IN HARMONY

The early human beings were hunter-gatherers, who lived in harmony with their environment.
They wandered across the countryside collecting leaves, wild fruits, nuts and seeds to eat, killing the occasional animal to supplement their diet.
They had little effect on their environment since there were few of them and they were constantly moving in search of new sources of food. Some tribal people in South America, Africa, Asia and Australia still live like this, but most people now live a settled life, mostly in towns and cities, producing a big impact on their environment.

HUMAN ECOLOGY & IMPACT

Two-thirds of the Earth's surface is covered by oceans and seas. Much of the remaining land is made up of mountains, deserts and polar regions — places that are difficult for people to live in. People need food, homes, clothes, fuels and other materials, which come directly or indirectly from the land. Today, the land is under pressure from an ever-increasing human population. In 1650 the world population was only 500 million; today there are more than 6 billion of us on Earth, creating pollution, desertification and the destruction of wildlife and wildlife habitats.

LADYBIRDS & APHIDS

The small, brightly-coloured ladybird is the most familiar of beetles and also one of the most helpful to farmers and gardeners. The adult beetles and their grubs feed mostly on aphids and are important in keeping these insect pests in check. A fully-grown grub can eat about 50 aphids a day. Nowadays some gardeners and farmers are actually introducing ladybirds to their crops to allow them to control aphids and other insect pests. This is called biological control.

POWER STATION
Power stations and factories pollute the air, producing acid rain and causing global warming. They also pollute rivers, lakes and the sea.

BUILDING WORK
As the human population continues to increase, more and more houses are being built on greenfield sites.

MOTOR VEHICLES
As well as causing noise, motor vehicles produce exhaust fumes which add to acid rain and global warming.

SPRAYING PESTICIDES
Farmers often spray their crops with pesticides and fertilizers. These may harm wildlife and also contaminate human food and drinking water.

A LOAD OF RUBBISH
Rubbish is unsightly and poses a danger to people and wildlife. It is also a waste of valuable resources, since much of it could be recycled.

ECOLOGISTS & ECOLOGY TODAY

STUDYING PLANT LIFE IN A TROPICAL RAINFOREST

If we are to understand and save the remaining rainforests, we have to know what lives there. This is not easy when many of the animals feed high in the trees, which are often 30 metres (100 ft) or more high. Ecologists now have to use some of the equipment of rock-climbers, including climbing irons, ropes and harnesses, to get close to the plants and animals high in the tree canopy. Often they build walkways from the top of one tree to the next.

The German biologist Ernst Haeckel first used the word 'oecology' in 1866, describing the study of living things and the way they interacted with the world around them. The modern spelling of ecology was not used until 1893. Since those days, ecology has progressed from the recording and describing of living things in their natural surroundings to a complex study that calls on all aspects of science, mathematics, computer science and statistics to provide detailed and accurate measurements about the environment and the living things in it. Today, ecology and ecologists are more necessary than ever to predict and measure the impact of human activities on the environment.

REINTRODUCING ANIMALS

The sea eagle is a magnificent bird of prey that became extinct in the British Isles in 1916. In 1975, after many years of study of the birds' habitat and life history in other countries, British ecologists released imported sea eagle chicks on an island off the west coast of Scotland. After a very slow start, the birds began to nest and breed, spreading out to other parts of Scotland. By 2000 there were 23 pairs of sea eagles in western Scotland and the total number of chicks reared by them had reached 100.

ECOLOGISTS IN ANTARCTICA

The polar regions are the last true wilderness left on Earth, but even here changes to the environment are taking place. Pipelines now carry oil and gas across the frozen land of the Arctic, while increasing numbers of cruise ships take tourists to Antarctica. Ecologists are busy studying the effects of these changes. In Antarctica ecologists from many countries work side by side to study penguins, seals, whales and other wildlife on that continent.

RECORDING FISH LIFE

Although ecologists now use many modern electronic and scientific devices to help them in their work, much of their work still involves careful observation on land and under water. These ecologists are measuring and examining pike from a local lake. Their results will be fed into a computer and analysed when they get back to the laboratory. Such analysis will save hundreds of hours of tedious calculations.

CULTURING RARE PLANTS

Some plants are extremely rare and attempts are being made to grow them in the laboratory so that eventually they can be returned to the wild. Many rare plants are difficult to grow from seeds, and ecologists have developed a way of producing new plants from a minute fragment in a test-tube containing a special jelly. This technique works well with some rare orchids and it means that many new plants can be grown from just one parent.

SCIENCE EXPLAINED: BOMB CALORIMETERS

One of the most important techniques now used by ecologists involves measuring the amount of energy passing along the various food chains in an ecosystem, using an instrument called a bomb calorimeter. A sample of plant or animal material is put inside the 'bomb' of the calorimeter, which is then sealed up. The piece of plant or animal is burnt and the increase in temperature is measured. This is converted to an energy measurement in joules or kilojoules. Because of such studies we now know that only about 10 per cent of energy is passed from one link in a food chain to the next.

GLOSSARY

Biodiversity – The variety of life on Earth

Biological control – The use of natural predators instead of chemicals to control other species

Biomes – Areas of the world characterized by their climate and plant life

Boom – A floating barrier used to prevent oil spreading out after a large spillage

Canopy – The top layer of a tropical rainforest

Carnivore – An animal that eats other animals

Classification – The process by which ecologists sort animals with similar characteristics into groups

Culturing – The growing of plants in the laboratory from fragments of a parent plant

Decomposer – An animal that completely breaks down dead plants and animals, releasing chemicals that other living things can use again

Detrivores – An animal that feeds on dead remains, breaking them down into smaller pieces

Ecosystem – The interaction between plants, animals and the environment in which they live

Exhaustion – The overworking of a habitat to the extent where it can no longer sustain any life

Habitat – A place where a group of organisms live

Herbivore – A plant-eating animal

Invertebrate – An animal without a backbone

Niche – A highly specialized habitat within an ecosystem

Predator – An animal or plant that preys on other animals

Productivity – The rate at which living things grow and breed

Photosynthesis – The method by which plants use sunlight to get their energy from water and carbon dioxide

Sensitive indicator species – Delicate species monitored by ecologists to ascertain the condition of a habitat

Stomata – Tiny holes in plant leaves that let carbon dioxide in and oxygen and water out

Succession – A change in nature where one set of plant and animal species disappear from a habitat and are succeeded by another

Vertebrate – An animal with a backbone

ACKNOWLEDGEMENTS

We would like to thank Advocate and Elizabeth Wiggans for their assistance.
Illustrations by Cy Baker, John Alston and Simon Mendez.
Copyright © 2001 *ticktock* Publishing Ltd.
First published in Great Britain by ticktock Publishing Ltd., Century Place, Lamberts Road, Tunbridge Wells, Kent TN2 3EH, U.K. All rights reserved.
No part of this publication may be reproduced, stored in a retrieval system, or transmitted in any form or by any means electronic, mechanical, photocopying, recording or otherwise, without prior written permission of the copyright owner.
A CIP catalogue record for this book is available from the British Library. ISBN 1 86007 257 7 (paperback). ISBN 1 86007 261 5 (hardback).

Printed in Malta 123456789

c=centre, l=left, r=right, OFC=outside front cover, IFC=inside front cover, IBC=inside back cover, OBC=outside back cover

ATG: 4t. Ardea: 19c, 22-23c, 23b. Bruce Coleman Collection: 6tl, 8t, 12tl, 12-13c, 14b, 16b, 17tr, 20l, 22tl, 22b & OBC. Corbis Images: 14-15c., 17c, 24t, 24cl, 24-25c, 25tr & OBC, 25cr, 26-27b, 27b, 28t, 28c, 30cl, 31t, 31c. Ecoscene: 19t. Environmental Images: 6-7c, 16t, 26t. The Enivronmental Picture Library: 7r, 18b. FLPA: 3t, 8b, 21t, 24b, 27tl. Terry Jennings: 2c, 14c, 18t. Oxford Scientific Films: 2tl, 2b. Science Photo Library: OFC. Still Pictures: 3b, 9c, 17br.

Every effort has been made to trace the copyright holders and we apologize in advance for any unintentional omissions.
We would be pleased to insert the appropriate acknowledgement in any subsequent edition of this publication.

snapping-turtle
guide

INDEX